Happy Mother's D[...]

We are very proud [...]

your role as a "m[...]

Mom & Dad 2005

D0406873

Just Moms

Just
Moms

A mother by any other squawk, cheep, yip, or mew is still as sweet

compiled by

Bonnie Louise Kuchler

Willow Creek®
PRESS

Published by Willow Creek Press
P.O. Box 147, Minocqua, Wisconsin 54548

Design: Pat Linder
Production Design: Lisa Moore
Editor: Andrea Donner

Library of Congress Cataloging-in-Publication Data
Just moms : a mother by any other squawk, cheep, yip, or mew is still as sweet / compiled by Bonnie Louise Kuchler.
     p. cm.
  ISBN 1-57223-504-7 (hardcover : alk. paper)
 1. Mothers--Quotations, maxims, etc. 2. Motherhood--Quotations, maxims, etc. I. Kuchler, Bonnie Louise.
  PN6084.M6 J87 2001
  306.874'3--dc21
                                                  2001003685

Printed in Canada

For Mom,
from your cub

Macaques © Erwin and Peggy Bauer

Acknowledgments

Special thanks to my husband Phillip Kuchler—
for laughing at the right parts of the book;
to my mom Betty Trakimas—
for sighing at the right parts of the book;
to my daughter Jill Sikes; my son Nate Sikes;
and my step-daughter, Laura Kuchler—
for editing out the right parts of the book.

Thanks to author-photographer, Becky Grambo;
freelance copy-editor, Kevin Miller;
and digital imaging technician, Kai Davis—
for helping me with the technical parts of the book.

And deeply felt thanks to an outstanding editor,
Andrea Donner—without whom there would
be no parts of the book.

Making the decision to have a child—it's momentous.
It is to decide forever to have your heart
go walking outside your body.

Elizabeth Stone
American author
As quoted in the *Village Voice*, 1981

*Of all the rights of women,
the greatest is to be a mother.*

Lin Yutang (1895-1976)
Chinese-born American author

The moment a child is born,
the mother is also born.
She never existed before.
The woman existed, but the mother, never.
A mother is something absolutely new.

Bhagwan Shree (Osho) Rajneesh (1931-1990)
Indian author

*That first little cry is mightier
than the cheers of ten thousand people.*

Anonymous

Ten-day-old grizzly bear cub nestled in mother's fur © Leonard Lee Rue III

*It's the mother
who can cure the child's tears*

African proverb

Bonobo mother kissing baby © John Giustina / Adventure Photo and Film

The purest thing I know in all earth's holding
is mother love, her precious child enfolding. . . .

Anonymous

Mother love is the cream of love.

Grecian proverb

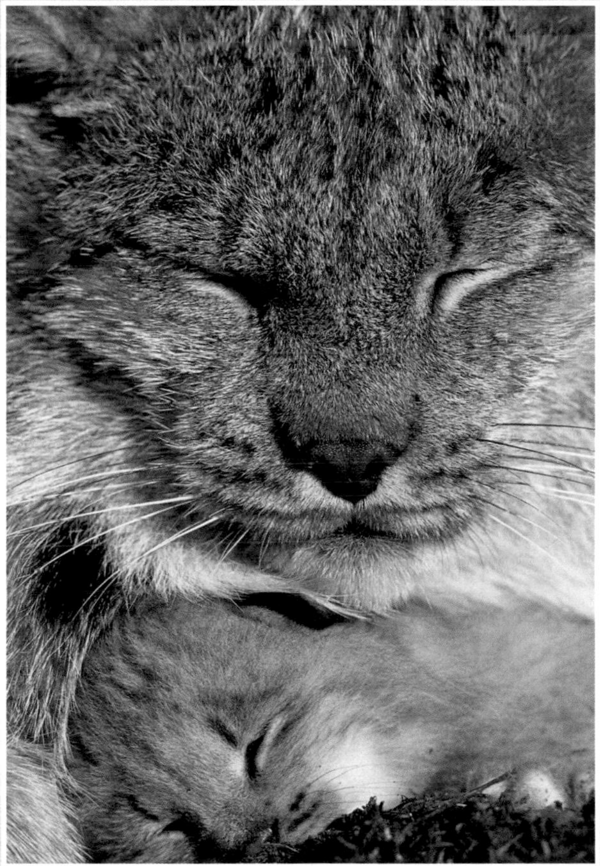

Canada lynx and kitten © Lisa & Mike Husar / Team Husar

*Who is getting more pleasure
from this rocking,
the baby or me?*

Nancy Thayer
American author

Orangutan mother and baby in Borneo rain forest © Daniel J. Cox / Natural Exposures, Inc.

Kissing the baby touches the mother.

Thai proverb

Giraffe and young, South Africa © Steve Bloom

Mother's arms are made of tenderness,
and sweet sleep blesses the child who lies therein.

Victor Hugo (1802-1885)
French author

The watchful mother tarries nigh,
though sleep has closed her infant's eyes.

John Keble (1792-1866)
English poet

People who say they sleep like a baby usually don't have one.

Leo J. Burke

Wolf pup greeting its mother, Montana © Lisa & Mike Husar / Team Husar

*Baby: A loud noise at one end
and no sense of responsibility at the other.*

Ronald Arbuthnott Knox (1888-1957)
English author, priest

There are times when parenthood seems nothing more than feeding the mouth that bites you.

Peter De Vries (1910-1993)
American author

When my kids become wild and unruly,
I use a nice, safe playpen.
When they're finished, I climb out.

Erma Bombeck (1927-1996)

A toddler believes that if you love a person,
you stay with that person 100 percent of the time.

Lawrence Balter
American author

*The fundamental job of a toddler
is to rule the universe.*

Lawrence Kutner
American author

Dall sheep kid on mother's back, Alaska © Michio Hoshino / Minden Pictures

You can learn many things from children.
How much patience you have, for instance.

Franklin Pierce Jones (1887-1929)
President and CEO of American Management Association

Lioness and cubs, East Africa © Franz Lanting / Minden Pictures

You will always be your child's favorite toy.

Vicki Lansky
American author

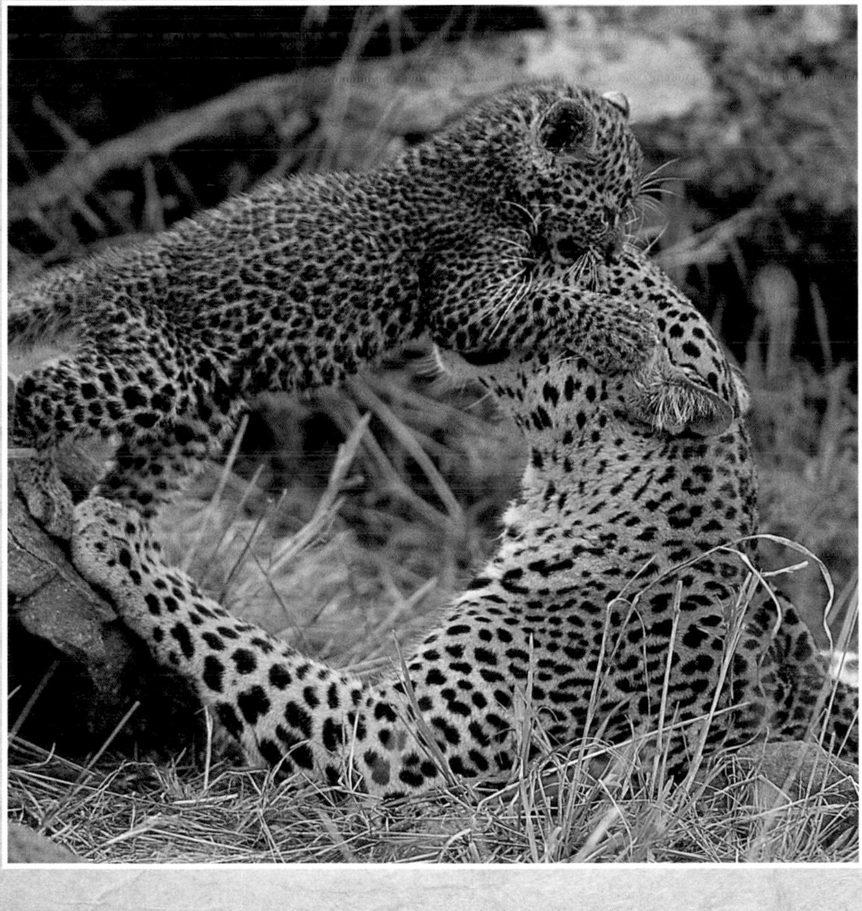

Leopard mother and cub, Kenya © Joe McDonald

There is no such thing as a non-working mother.

Hester Mundis
American author

Any mother could perform the jobs
of several air-traffic controllers with ease.

Lisa Alther
American author

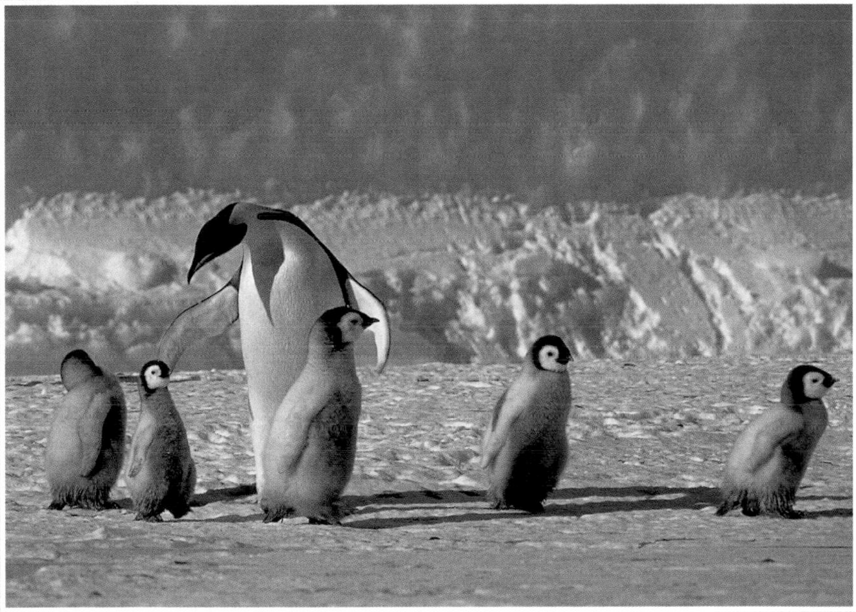

Emperor penguin © ARDEA LONDON / G. Robertson

All mothers have intuition.
The great ones have radar.

Cathy Guisewite
American cartoonist

*Sometimes the strength of motherhood
is greater than natural laws.*

Barbara Kingsolver
American author

For the mother is and must be,
whether she knows it or not,
the greatest, strongest
and most lasting teacher her children have.

Hannah Whitall Smith (1832-1911)

Children are natural mimics
who act like their parents
despite every effort to teach them good manners.

Anonymous

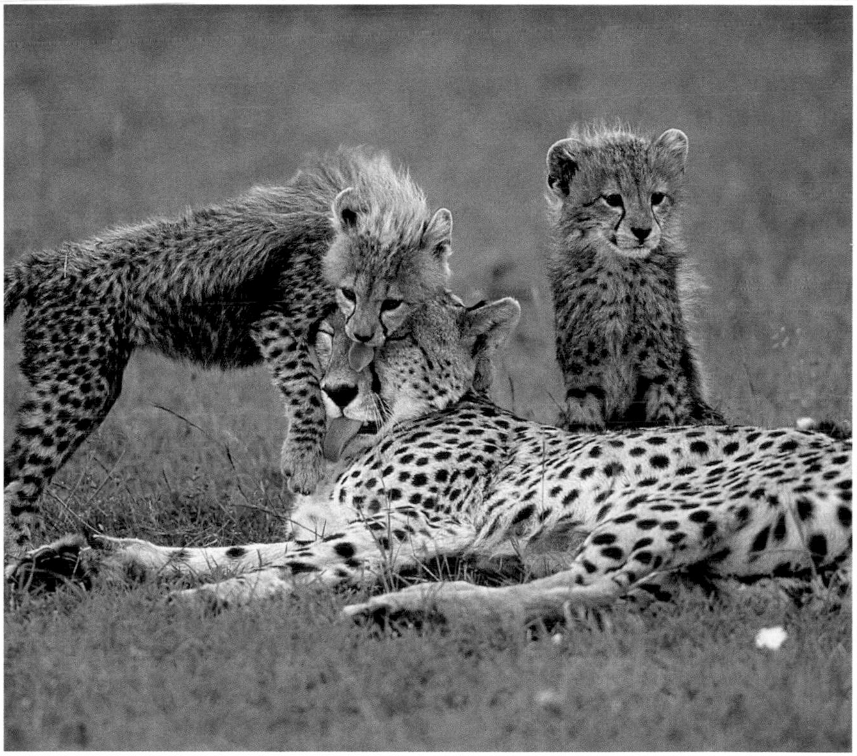

Cheetah and cubs, Kenya © Art Wolfe

Where there's a will there's a way,
and where there's a child there's a will.

Marcelene Cox
American writer

Grizzly bear mother with cub, northern Rockies © Erwin and Peggy Bauer

*The toughest thing about raising kids
is convincing them that you have seniority.*

Gene Brown
American author

*I have found that the best way
to give advice to your children
is to find out what they want
and then advise them to do it.*

Harry S. Truman (1884-1972)

Elk cow sniffing calf's ear in meadow © Daniel J. Cox / Natural Exposures, Inc.

In raising my children
I have lost my mind but found my soul.

Anonymous

*No matter how calmly you try to referee,
parenting will eventually produce bizarre behavior,
and I'm not talking about the kids.
Their behavior is always normal.*

Bill Cosby

Sumatran orangutan mother and baby © Steve Bloom

True, a mother has many cares
but they are sweet cares.

Juliette Montague Cooke (1812-1896)
Teacher of children of royalty in Hawaii

The heart of a mother is a deep abyss
at the bottom of which
you will always find forgiveness.

Honoré de Balzac (1799-1850)
French author

Emperor penguin with chick, Antarctica © ANIMALS ANIMALS / Johnny Johnson

A mother understands what a child does not say.

Jewish proverb

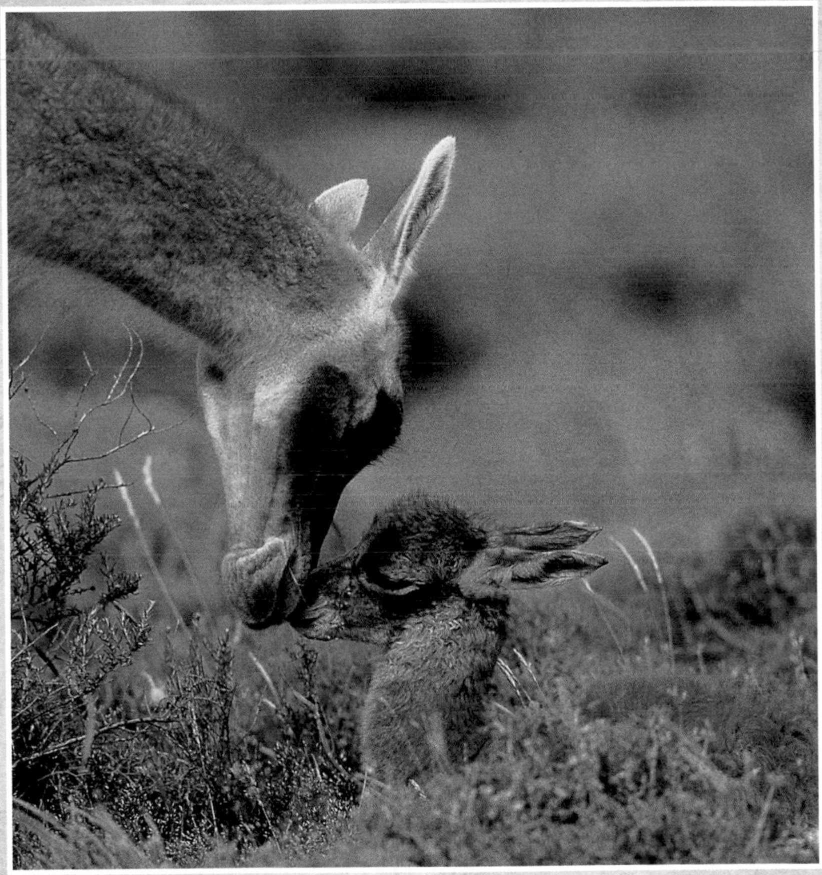

Llamas, Torres Del Paine National Park, Chile © Art Wolfe

They say there is no other
can take the place of mother.

George Bernard Shaw (1856-1950)
Ireland-born, English playwright

Mother fox and cub © Wendy Shattil / Bob Rozinski

There is only one beautiful child in the world and every mother has it.

Chinese proverb

A mother is the truest friend we have,
when trials, heavy and sudden, fall upon us . . .
still will she cling to us,
and endeavor by her kind precepts and counsels
to dissipate the clouds of darkness,
and cause peace to return to our hearts.

Washington Irving (1783-1859)
American author

A mother's love endures through all.

Washington Irving (1783-1859)
American author

Baby orangutan on mother's shoulders, Borneo © Steve Bloom

Mother's presence is like a fixed light
that gives the child the security
to move out safely to explore the world
and then return safely to harbour.

Louise J. Kaplan
American author

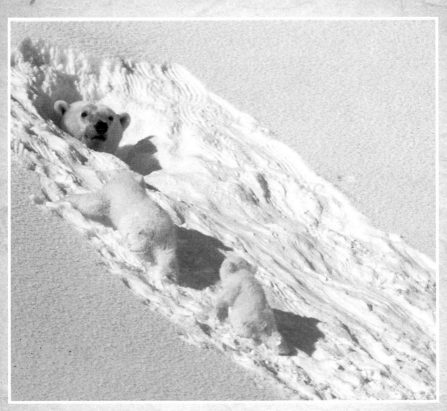

Life, love, and laughter—
what priceless gifts to give our children.

Phyllis Campbell Dryden
American writer

Bonobo and young © Steve Bloom

A mother is a person who,
seeing there are only four pieces of pie for five people,
promptly announces she never did care for pie.

Anonymous

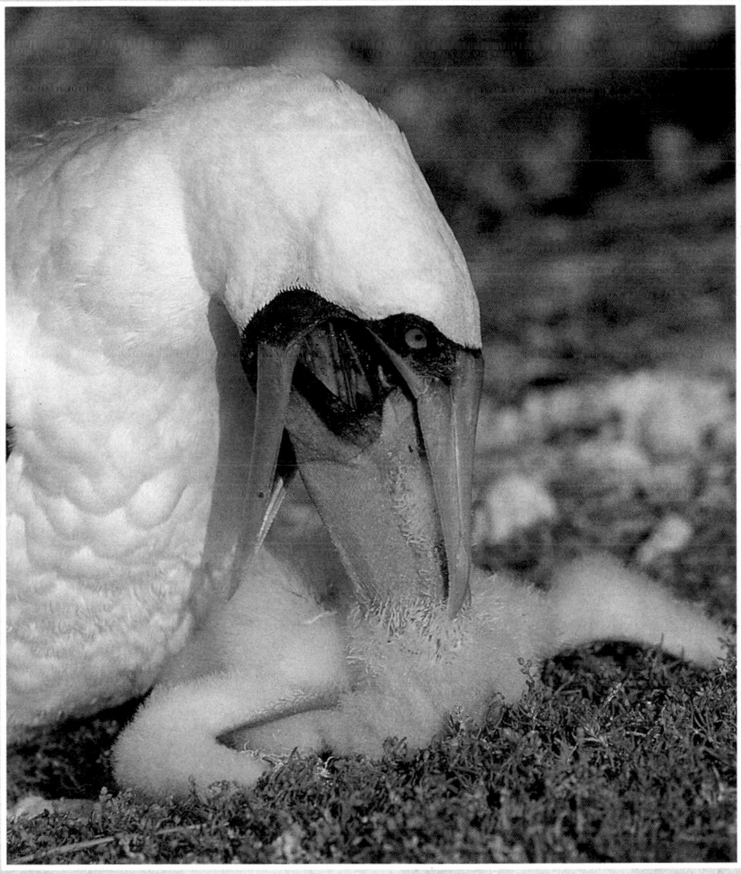

Masked booby feeds chick © Erwin and Peggy Bauer

*Be generous with your child's needs
and conservative with her wants.
More importantly, know the difference.*

Anonymous

King penguin and adult chick, Falkland Islands © Joe McDonald

A mother is not a person to lean on
but a person to make leaning unnecessary.

Dorothy Canfield Fisher (1879-1958)
American author

Great people are those who make others feel
that they, too, can become great.

Mark Twain (1835-1910)

Grizzly with four-month-old cubs, Washington © Erwin and Peggy Bauer

A mother's children are portraits of herself.

Anonymous

Mother cheetah and cubs © Daniel J. Cox / Natural Exposures, Inc.

Where children are, there is the golden age.

Novalis (1772-1801)
German poet

Time spent with your family doing ordinary things is the most extraordinary time of all.

Jan Blaustone
American author

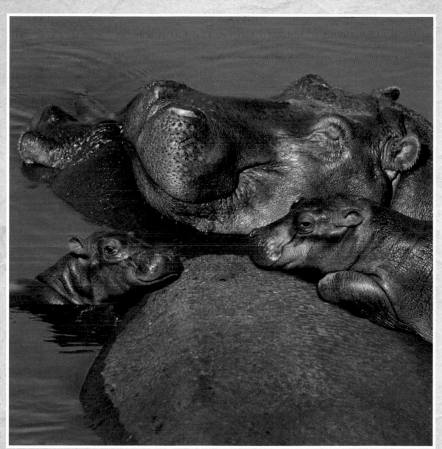

Hippo family resting, Masai Mara, Kenya © Steve Bloom

*There are only two lasting bequests
we can hope to give our children.
One is roots; the other, wings.*

Hodding Carter, Jr. (1907-1972)
American journalist and author

Emperor penguin with chick © Art Wolfe

Mothers hold their children's hands
for just a little while,
their hearts forever.

Anonymous

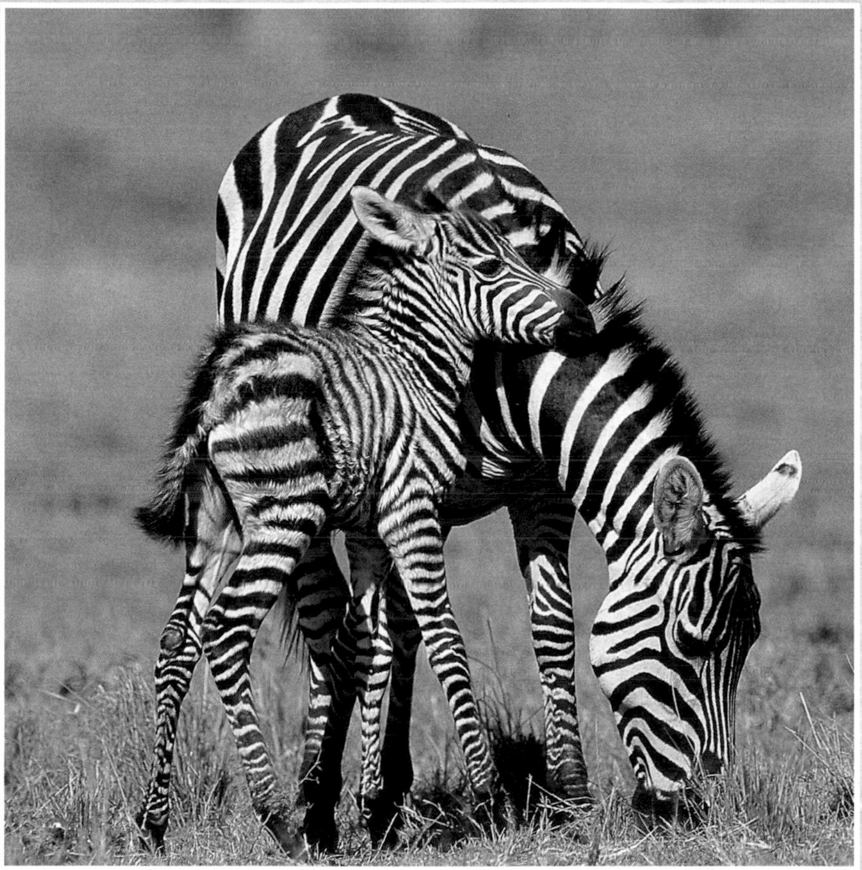

Zebra and baby, Masai Mara, Kenya © Joe McDonald

Hold your child's hand now,
while you still can.

Anonymous

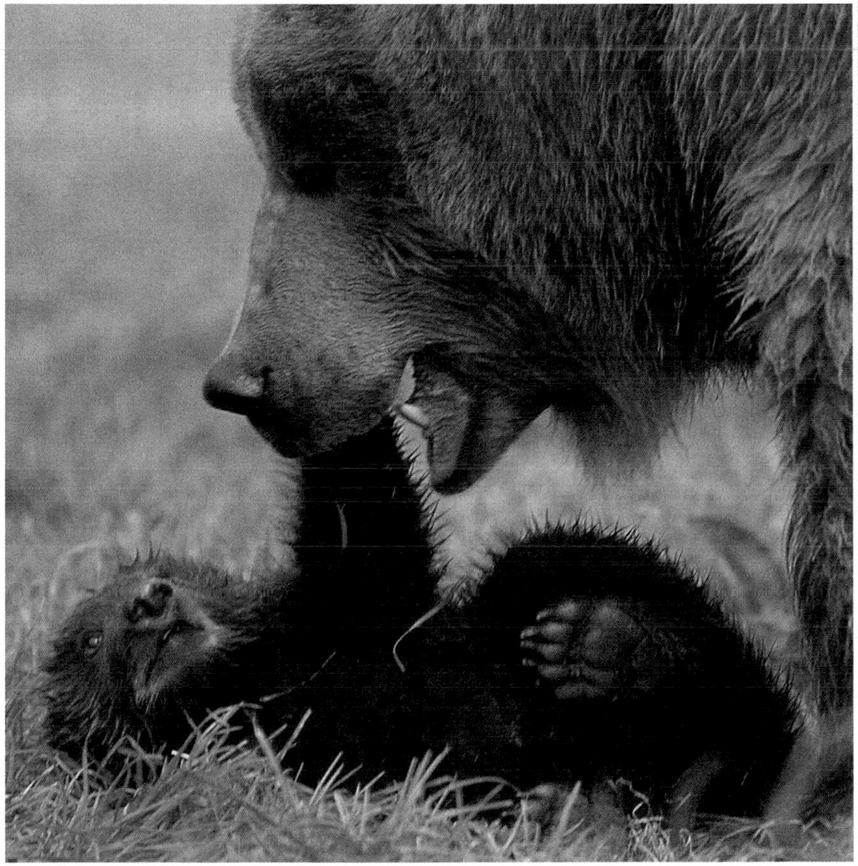

Grizzly mother plays with cub © Erwin and Peggy Bauer

The best things in life aren't things.

Anonymous

Bibliography

Grateful acknowledgment is made to the authors and publishers for use of the following material. Every effort has been made to contact original sources. If notified, the publisher will be pleased to rectify an omission in future editions.

Adler, Bill [compiled by]. *Motherhood: A Celebration*. New York: Carroll & Graf Publishers, 1997.

Balter, Lawrence, with Anita Shreve. *Who's In Control?: Dr. Balter's Guide to Discipline Without Combat*. New York: Poseidon Press, 1989.

Bernard, Jessie. *The Future of Motherhood*. New York: Dial Press, 1974.

Blaustone, Jan. *The Joy of Parenthood: Inspiration and Encouragement for Parents*. Deephaven, MN: Meadowbrook Press; New York: distributed by Simon & Schuster, 1993.

Cosby, Bill. *Fatherhood; introduction and afterword by Alvin F. Poussaint*. Garden City, NY: Doubleday, 1986.

De Vries, Peter. *Tunnel of Love*. Boston: Little, Brown and Co., 1954.

Fisher, Dorothy Canfield. *Her Son's Wife*. New York: Harcourt, Brace and Company, 1926.

Kaplan, Louise J. *Oneness and Separateness: From Infant to Individual.* New York: Simon & Schuster, 1978.

Kutner, Lawrence. *Toddlers and Preschoolers.* New York: W. Morrow, 1994.

Lansky, Vicki. *Trouble-Free Travel with Children: Helpful Hints for Parents on the Go.* Book Peddlers, 1996.

Mieder, Wolfgang [compiled by]. *Illuminating Wit, Inspiring Wisdom: Proverbs from Around the World.* Paramus, NJ: Prentice Hall, 1998.

Phillips, Bob [compiled by]. *Phillips' Book of Great Thoughts, Funny Sayings: A Stupendous Collection of Quotes, Quips, Epigrams, Witticisms, and Humorous Comments: for Personal Enjoyment and Ready Reference.* Wheaton, IL: Tyndale House, 1993.

Quinn, Tracy, ed. *Quotable Women of the Twentieth Century: Introduction by Cathleen Black.* New York: W. Morrow, 1999.

The Speaker's Electronic Reference Collection, Aapex Software, 1994.

Sumrall, Amber Coverdale, ed. *Write to the Heart: Wit & Wisdom of Women Writers.* Freedom, CA: Crossing Press, 1992.

Thayer, Nancy. *Stepping.* Garden City, NY: Doubleday, 1980.

Zona, Guy A. [compiled by]. *True Love is Friendship Set on Fire: and Other Proverbs of Love.* New York: Simon & Schuster, 1998.